ANTONIO VIVALDI

Gloria

RV 589

arranged for SSA, trumpet in C, oboe, strings and organ

by Desmond Ratcliffe
The English version has been added by the arranger.

Order No: NOV 07 0445

NOVELLO PUBLISHING LIMITED

Dedicated to Janette R. Stewart and the
Girls' Choir of Balfron High School, Glasgow

ARRANGER'S NOTE

This arrangement was made from a microfilm of the original manuscript kindly supplied by the Biblioteca Nazionale, Turin.

Dynamics, and slurring where advisable, have been added, as Vivaldi's own markings were very few.

It is suggested in No. 7 that the rhythms ♩. ♪ and ♫ are sung as ♩.. ♪ and ♪. ♪ , shown respectively by ♮ and ⌐¬ over the quavers.

The tempo mark for No. 11 has been added in square brackets as none was given.

ORCHESTRATION

Trumpet in C

Oboe

Strings

Organ

Full score and parts are available on hire.

DURATION ABOUT 33 MINUTES

GLORIA
RV 589

Arranged for SSA,
with English version,
by Desmond Ratcliffe

ANTONIO VIVALDI
1678-1741

1 GLORIA IN EXCELSIS DEO

20273

6

2 ET IN TERRA PAX HOMINIBUS

20273

14

3 LAUDAMUS TE

A-dor - a - mus te, a-dor-a - mus
We a - dore thee, God, we a - dore thee,

te,
God,

Glo - ri-fi - ca - mus te.
We glo-ri - fy thee, Lord.

4 GRATIAS AGIMUS TIBI

5 PROPTER MAGNAM GLORIAM

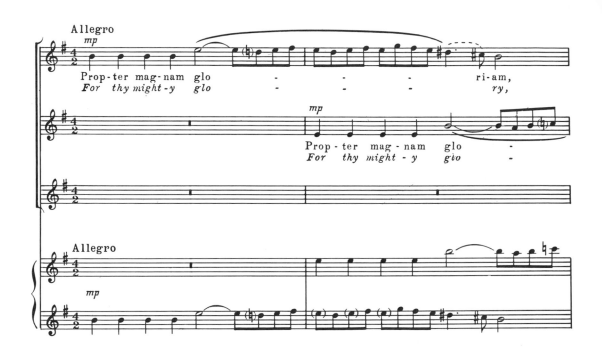

*Largo is given in the original, but this seems very slow.

32

20273

34

20273

7 DOMINE FILI UNIGENITE

* Original MS has D here in Tenor.

38

20278

42

* This F is original
† This E is original

20273

* This F is original
† This E is original
20273

8 DOMINE DEUS, AGNUS DEI

9 QUI TOLLIS PECCATA MUNDI

10 QUI SEDES AD DEXTERAM PATRIS

*The original has A♯ in the bass.

54

20273

mi - se - re - re, mi - se - re - re, mi - se -
Lord have mer-cy, Lord have mer - cy, Lord have

re - re___ no - bis.
mer - cy___ up - on us.

11 QUONIAM TU SOLUS SANCTUS

42

58

20273

12 CUM SANCTO SPIRITU

61

65

20273

66

67

20273

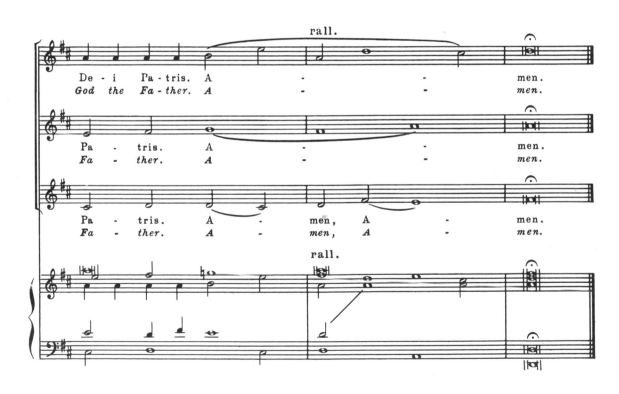

Novello Publishing Limited
Printed in Great Britain by Caligraving Limited, Thetford, Norfolk.